Networking for Underdogs

The Ambitionairy's Guide to Networking:
Big Dreams on a Small Budget

Soulaima Gourani

First published Soulaima Gourani - 2024

Copyright © 2024 Soulaima Gourani

All rights reserved. No part of this publication may be copied or reproduced in any form, by any means, electronic or otherwise, without prior consent from the copyright owner and publisher of this book.

First edition

Table of Contents

Introduction 4

Over the past 30 years, networking has evolved 6

What is networking? 8

Do you hoard knowledge or share it freely? 14

Networking stress 19

Next step - self-assessment 23

How to get people to help you repeatedly 29

"Giving" is the new "taking" 39

The 9 networking types and personalities 65

The art of introductions 90

As we reach the end of the book 96

Introduction

I'm a former street and foster care child who left home and was kicked out of school at just 13. Against all odds, I overcame the challenges thrown my way and became a recognized leader - featured in Thinkers50, named one of Europe's 40 Under 40, honored as a Young Global Leader by the World Economic Forum, recognized in Nordic20, and celebrated as one of the Top 100 Influential Women, among many other accolades.

Born in North Africa, I grew up in Denmark and later immigrated to the USA, where I am now the co-founder and CEO of a VC-funded AI tech startup. Since 2002, I have shared my strategies at prestigious institutions such as Harvard, Stanford, INCAE in Costa Rica, ISB in India, CBS, London Business School, INSEAD, and HULT, as well as with numerous Fortune 500 companies.

In this book, I'll share my step-by-step method for mastering networking on the smallest budget possible. You can implement these strategies from anywhere - no excuses. If you want to make an impact, remember networking is your key to success.

Here's the deal: you don't need to know hundreds of people to get things done or make an impact. Sometimes, all it takes is 12, 30, or maybe 50 key connections.

The big question is: who are those people? It's all about quality, not quantity.

I wish more folks would sit down and really evaluate their current network versus who they want to connect with. And let's be real - location or limited resources are not excusing anymore. You can network just as effectively online as you can in person.

So, I challenge you: dive into my book. It's straightforward and inexpensive to put into action. But remember, it's all about sticking to it - developing the routines and good habits that will help you succeed.

Let's make it happen!

Soulaima Gourani

Over the past 30 years, networking has evolved

What was once an exclusive privilege of the wealthy, famous, or naturally gifted is now open to everyone. But you still need to understand the strategies, the does and don'ts and have a proper toolbox to deal with deferent types of people (networking types).

Networking used to happen behind "closed doors," and you only had access if you came from the right family or held a certain job title that justified your membership in a club or lodge. Back then, it was more about keeping people out. Today, it's all about gaining access to the right opportunities.

This practical guide is designed to give you quick insights and tools, so you can start networking with purpose by tomorrow. You'll be introduced to the most effective tools and strategies that can help you tap into new knowledge, resources, customers, successful projects, investors, and maybe even land that new job.

This basic guide focuses on your personal network. While some experts say individual networks aren't that interesting, I disagree. You can't teach others, lead, or benefit from networking unless you know how to network yourself. The first step is becoming skilled at managing and leveraging your own network.

Think of your professional relationships as your personal property, your capital, and your market value. The company you work for is just borrowing your network - they don't own it. That's not to say businesses shouldn't work to unlock the hidden potential their employees bring with them.

This guide is for you if you:

- Need new inspiration and energy.
- Lack models or frameworks.
- Want to map out, nurture, and grow your network.
- Aim to be more professional in your approach to networking.
- Attend my talks or seminars.
- Are responsible for teaching others how to network.
- Feel like networking just isn't working for you.

What is Networking?

Networking is more than just the act of meeting people; it's the strategic engagement that fosters meaningful relationships and exchanges of value. Often misunderstood, networking is frequently cloaked in outdated stereotypes that suggest one must be ruthlessly ambitious or self-serving. Effective networking is a wellspring of joy, fulfillment, and personal growth.

In our interconnected society, your capacity to cultivate trusted, loyal relationships is essential for accessing knowledge, opportunities, and resources.

You're called to balance the depth of a specialist's expertise with the breadth of a generalist's perspective. Increasingly, the expectation is not just to possess knowledge but to engage in innovative problem-solving that transcends conventional thinking. Few of us thrive by working in isolation; it's crucial to facilitate group dynamics, fostering collaboration and knowledge sharing.

In a landscape of flattening hierarchies, the ability to inspire colleagues to take ownership and make swift, informed decisions is vital. Even the most exceptional talents must operate within the framework of community, as cross-industry collaboration and diverse perspectives are key competitive advantages.

As a leader, consider this: Would you prefer to hire someone who operates in a vacuum, or would you value someone capable of engaging collaboratively across departments and agendas? The most successful leaders seek out individuals who can swiftly align their unique complementary skills with the challenges at hand.

What is a network?

A network is not merely a collection of contacts; it embodies the relationships you cultivate with those around you. Your network is composed of individuals from whom you seek insights, inspiration, and support. It reflects the sum of your choices and decisions, nurturing your career and enriching your life. When you build a robust network of exceptionally talented individuals whose strengths complement your own, you can tackle more complex challenges with greater efficiency and effectiveness than you could alone.

Time is our most precious resource. A thoughtfully constructed and actively maintained network can significantly reduce wasted effort and maximize productivity. Embrace the power of connection and watch how it transforms your professional landscape.

Why should I network?

In my view, you must seize control of your network; otherwise, it will ultimately control you. Everyone has a network, but the real question is whether you have a clear understanding of it and are leveraging the myriad benefits it offers. Most of us accumulate random connections that evolve or fade over time. Would you work for a company without a strategy?

If you were headed to an unfamiliar place, wouldn't you bring a map? Networking is no different. Without a plan, you risk ending up anywhere. Throughout your life, you will encounter numerous opportunities, but not every opportunity is right for you. To identify the right one, you must be able to recognize it when it arrives.

Everyone networks

You can no longer afford to say you don't want to network. Networking is the fastest way to transform a significant problem into a manageable one or to turn a bad idea into a good one. Through your network, you become a Bermuda Triangle of knowledge. Knowledge is essential unless you're engaged in work that doesn't require your intellect. Whether you're an employee, student, entrepreneur, job seeker, or leader, YOU alone bear the responsibility for cultivating the right network.

You don't need to be the smartest person in the room; you just need to be genuinely interested in others and curious about how you can help each other. It is your responsibility to create a well-organized, competent, agile, and loyal network.

The networking cycle

Be cautious not to engage with your network only when you have a problem to solve. Continuously be present and available. This is the only way to establish and maintain the mutual trust and credibility that form the foundation of your network. Many people network reactively, seeking assistance only when in need, rather than proactively, as they should. Most are adept at initiating relationships, but few excel at optimizing and nurturing them. This often places them in a position where their motives are short-sighted, aiming to extract immediate value while neglecting the creation of long-term relationships that provide mutual benefits.

To network effectively, you need to understand the five stages a relationship goes through to become strong. All relationships begin at a specific time and place. From there, they must develop. You meet, engage in conversation, and perhaps connect on a virtual platform, such as LinkedIn, Facebook, or X. You might keep in touch over time, gradually fostering a deeper sense of connection and trust. Eventually, the relationship becomes more informal as you both feel increasingly comfortable in each other's presence.

Connection lifecycle

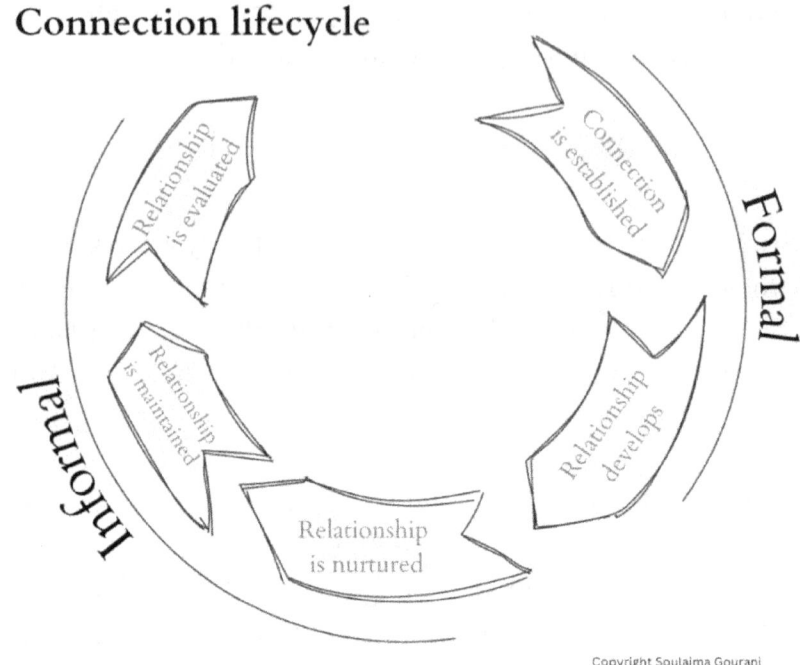

Do you inspire trust or distrust?

We network with individuals we personally trust. High personal trust influences our perception of others' professional capabilities and strengthens our professional confidence in them. Many of us place deep, almost blind faith in certain people within our networks, which can be counterproductive. Those you connect with should not only be trustworthy but also among the most competent in their fields - individuals who can complement, challenge, and inspire you. Your primal instincts often lead you to network with those you like and trust, rather than those who could genuinely push you to grow.

Whether people support you hinges on whether you are perceived as trustworthy or not. Do you know how others truly feel about you?

I encourage you to take stock of your network, to engage in structured and purposeful networking, and to optimize your resources effectively. Don't limit yourself to those you already know, chance encounters, or individuals with whom you feel a sense of camaraderie.

I know a woman who prefers to network only with those she enjoys being around and feels a strong connection with. Her network comprises good friends who are also colleagues. When her department was relocated, she was unable to follow and now needs support from colleagues in other departments to advocate for her skills. Unfortunately, her existing network could not assist because they were similarly limited to their closest working relationships. Other colleagues were not able to help, as they lacked personal and professional trust in her.

Does this story resonate with you? Always remember that your network is your social capital, the only guarantee you have for achieving your personal and professional goals.

Therefore, your network should be carefully curated, diligently nurtured, and regularly assessed. Avoid confining your networking to local or professionally narrow and comfortable circles.

Do you hoard knowledge or share it freely?

Reflecting on your school days, consider this: Were you the type who willingly let others copy your homework, or did you closely guard your answers? If you resonate with the latter, it indicates a significant challenge you might face in networking as an adult. This attitude - of protecting your work and not sharing - often reflects deeper characteristics that can hinder your professional growth.

As children, we often view sharing knowledge as a potential threat to our success. The fear of losing our edge or being overshadowed can make us protective of our efforts. However, this mindset can carry over into adulthood, where collaboration and knowledge sharing are essential for thriving in a networked world.

I once taught MBA students at the Indian School of Business, and when I posed the question of whether they would ever consider sharing their homework with classmates, they were shocked at the notion of allowing someone to copy their work. This reaction highlights a common belief: that sharing knowledge diminishes personal value or competitive advantage.

Yet, in the world of business and networking, the opposite is true. The most successful individuals understand that collaboration and generosity build stronger connections. Sharing knowledge fosters trust and creates an environment where everyone can grow. Instead of viewing sharing as a risk, see it as an investment in your network. By helping others succeed, you enhance your own reputation and open doors to new opportunities. In essence, the protective attitude you developed in school can limit your potential.

Embracing a mindset of generosity not only enriches your relationships but also paves the way for greater collaboration, innovation, and success in your career. Remember, in networking, it's not just about what you can gain; it's about what you can give and how that fosters a thriving community.

Innovative, growth-oriented companies increasingly focus on how to motivate individuals to share knowledge. Those who merely exchange information do not engage in true networking. Knowledge sharing only occurs between individuals who trust one another - both personally and professionally.

For a company, having employees who withhold their knowledge is perilous. Yet many organizations still view networking as a private affair, missing out on vast potential. In my experience, companies, leaders, and employees who systematically develop their skills in establishing, managing, and evaluating relationships outperform those who neglect this crucial aspect. None of us work in isolation anymore; we all rely, in one way or another, on others to support, contribute to, market, or develop our services and products.

At Copenhagen Business School (CBS), where I pursued my e-MBA, I adopted a simple yet powerful philosophy: every semester, I made my assignments and insights available to the next cohort of students.

This wasn't just about being generous; it was a strategic choice. Years later, when I returned to CBS as a guest lecturer, I was struck by how many students already knew my name and my work. They had engaged with the very materials I had shared, and this created a connection that enriched my teaching experience, and network with the next generation.

Knowledge is like capital; it must be deployed to create value. When you share what you learn, you don't just help others - you expand your influence and build a network of advocates who appreciate your contributions. It's a virtuous cycle.

Think about it: organizations that foster a culture of knowledge-sharing and collaboration, often outperform their competitors. They thrive because they understand that innovation is fueled by diverse perspectives and open dialogue.

Networking isn't about what you can take; it's about what you can give. When you approach it with this mindset, you transform relationships from transactional to transformational.

What is your currency?

Every time you meet someone, they're assessing you. They're weighing whether you're worth their time or not. Sadly, but true!

We all instinctively gauge one another; this is just human nature. The real question is: Do you know what people are looking for?

They're looking for:

- **Your Personality:** Do you spark their curiosity? Do you inspire trust? Is there a genuine connection?
- **Your Current Power Base:** Who is in your existing network? Are you well-connected?
- **Your Present and Future Skills:** Do you show potential? Are you perceived as a "rising star"?

We all aspire to be the person others want to engage with - someone they admire, recommend, and connect with.

This desire is completely natural, but it's essential to recognize that not everyone will want to connect with you. You're a complex human being with unique strengths and challenges, and that means you can't be everything to everyone; otherwise, you risk being nothing to anyone.

Take a moment to reflect on your values, your personal brand, and your strengths. Strive to be someone people are eager to recommend by doing the following:

- **Work on yourself:** Commit to becoming the best, most authentic version of yourself - always.

- **Help others succeed:** Be genuinely invested in the success of others, even if it means stepping back to let them shine.
- **Share your knowledge:** Understand that sharing your insights and experiences benefits both you and those around you.
- **Invite engagement:** Be open to others influencing your life, thoughts, and perspectives.
- **Be an interesting conversationalist:** Aim to inspire others through engaging discussions and authentic interactions.
- **Choose your networking platforms wisely:** Be selective about the environments and forums in which you connect, ensuring they align with your goals.

Remember, your true currency is not just what you know but how you share it and the value you create in your connections. By cultivating meaningful relationships and continuously investing in yourself, you position yourself as a trusted resource in your network, paving the way for mutual success.

Networking stress

After meetings, conferences, or travels, many find themselves overwhelmed by a mountain of business cards/social media invites and requests.

They feel a sense of stress when staring at this pile, knowing that others expect an email, an invitation, a virtual call, or a coffee meeting.

The thought of going out to meet new people can evoke a sense of dread, discouraging many from exchanging business cards in the first place. Those who do attend events often leave feeling disillusioned, having bounced from endless dinners, coffee dates, and conferences without reaping any rewards from their invested time. Many are wasting time and resources.

The good news? You can do something about it - and it's relatively straightforward. Essentially, you can take the following steps:

- Recognize that you don't need to know a lot of people to succeed. This is a common misconception about being a good networker. It's not about quantity; it's about quality. You might only need to connect with 12, 43, or 67 people. Many believe they must step outside their normal routines (taking time away from their personal lives) to network effectively. That doesn't have to be the case. Networking simply means doing what you already do, but better and more intentionally. You already encounter people in your workplace, on the bus, or while waiting in line.

- Learn to optimize your time with others so that you can get to know them quickly and effectively.
- Make a conscious effort to connect with people who have fewer than four commonalities with you. This ensures you don't just echo each other's thoughts and opinions.

Are you feeling stressed from networking? Many experience what I term "networking stress." You can avoid this by simply:

- Setting clear goals for why you want to network - so you know your motivations.
- Identifying whom you want to connect with - to ensure you're spending your precious time wisely.
- Choosing the methods that resonate with you - so your approach aligns with your natural inclinations.
- Continuously evaluating your relationships - to keep everything calibrated.

You can network anywhere

Networking can happen spontaneously - in a bus, on a plane, in a store, or while waiting in line. You can also network in a planned manner, such as attending a scheduled course, conference, or meeting. You can engage physically or virtually.

Physical networking occurs when you're in the same space as others. Being in a room full of people doesn't automatically equate to effective networking. To make the most of face-to-face interactions, you need to know what and who you want to network with, how you can assist others, and what value you bring to the table.

Virtual networking is, by nature, when you engage with people online. The conversation currently revolves around the use of Web 2.0 tools. You're likely familiar with platforms like Facebook, LinkedIn, and X. These are relevant forums that you should explore; they are excellent for nurturing your relationships. However, they shouldn't be your primary networking strategy. Instead, integrate them as part of your overall networking plan, which should also prioritize physical contact.

The key is to maintain a clear overview of who you know, how well you know them, and whether your relationships are sustainable. Networking is about understanding who you know, who you should know, and how to improve your access to them. You need tools to map, nurture, and expand your relationships with those who can inspire, develop, and assist you in your professional life.

You require both physical and virtual interactions. My experience has shown that if you've met someone in person, it's easier to maintain virtual contact than if you've only had a "web-only" relationship. People still crave face-to-face meetings and the ability to read one another to foster the necessary trust.

What is strategic networking?

Strategic networking encompasses the thoughts and actions you undertake to map out who you know, nurture your existing relationships, and expand your connections to those you don't yet know but would like to meet. Contrary to popular belief, strategic networking isn't more time-consuming; in fact, it's quite the opposite.

Fast or slow networking?

Many individuals approach networking with a transactional, commercial mindset. It's akin to the difference between fast food and slow food. Fast food represents quick networking: it fills you up but only for a short while. Before long, you're off in search of new connections to achieve that sense of "fullness" again. When you network in a "fast" manner, those relationships rarely return; they seldom reach out after meeting you, and if they do, they rarely recommend you to others.

On the other hand, if you network as if you're savoring slow food, you prioritize quality over quantity. The entire experience of developing the relationship takes center stage, not just the act of consuming connections. In slow networking, you take your time getting to know someone, allowing you to tailor your approach to their unique needs and expectations.

Next step - self-assessment

I can't stress this enough: do a self-assessment. The minute you start believing your own excuses, that's when the wheels start to come off. You need to stay ruthlessly honest about who you are and how you network.

Take a good, hard look at your approach. What do you do well, and where do you stumble? Examine your relationships: Who are the people your vibe with effortlessly? Who feels like a drag? And let's be real - do folks follow up after your meetings, or do they ghost you? Be your own toughest critic. That baseline assessment isn't just important; it's essential. Once you have clarity, you can start building the kind of network that serves you.

Reflecting on your life is crucial for personal and professional growth. It's not merely nostalgia; it's about gaining clarity and understanding your interactions. Your character is shaped by your choices and the sum of your routines and habits. To become more successful and fulfilled, you need to scrutinize these elements closely.

Just as a well-engineered product requires intentional design, so does a meaningful life. Evaluate whether your daily habits align with your long-term goals.

1. **Take time to examine your daily routines and choices.** What habits serve you well, and which ones hinder your progress? This reflection can reveal areas for improvement and help you cultivate more intentional behaviors.

2. **Recognizing patterns:** Pay attention to recurring themes in your life. Are there specific biases that influence your decision-making? Acknowledging these patterns allows you to break free from limiting beliefs and embrace new perspectives.

3. **Challenging assumptions:** Often, we hold onto biases without questioning them. Reflecting on these assumptions can open doors to diverse viewpoints and enrich your understanding of the world. It's a chance to challenge the status quo and engage in more meaningful conversations.

4. **Embracing change:** Life is inherently dynamic, and the ability to adapt is crucial. Reflecting on your experiences can help you identify the lessons learned from challenges and setbacks, equipping you with the resilience to navigate future uncertainties.

5. **Cultivating curiosity:** Approach your reflections with curiosity. What have you learned from your experiences? How can those insights inform your future actions? This mindset fosters continuous growth and innovation.

6. **Setting intentional goals:** Use your reflections to set clear, actionable goals that align with your values. By understanding

what truly matters to you, you can focus your efforts on what will bring you fulfillment and success.

7. **Building relationships:** Finally, reflect on how your habits and biases impact your relationships. Are there ways to improve your interactions with others? Cultivating empathy and understanding can lead to stronger, more authentic connections.

8. **Dare to ask:** Don't hesitate to reach out to trusted individuals in your life for their perspectives. Sometimes, our self-doubt, imposter syndrome, and inner critics cloud our view of our strengths and achievements. Their insights can illuminate aspects of yourself you might overlook, helping you recognize the good that you bring to the table.

Ultimately, taking the time to reflect allows you to navigate life more intentionally, leveraging your insights to foster growth, adaptability, and a much deeper connections with others. It's a continuous journey of self-discovery that can profoundly shape your personal and professional journey.

Do people really care?

How can you tell if someone is genuinely interested in you? Building a solid network and strong relationships takes time. Patience is key. Hold off on asking for favors or advice until you feel the relationship is strong enough to support it. Sure, being proactive is great, but be mindful not to come on too strong.

Remember, just because someone is polite doesn't mean they're inviting further engagement. Read between the lines to see if they're truly interested in you.

Here are some observations that guide my approach:

1. **Response time matters.** If I reach out and receive a quick reply, that's a positive sign.

2. **Engagement is key.** When I ask for a call or a meeting, if they respond within two days with a positive answer and suggest specific times, it shows they value the connection.

3. **Follow-through counts.** If they keep our commitments and follow up with gratitude, it reflects their interest in the relationship.

4. **Mutual dialogue is essential.** When we talk, there should be an equal exchange of ideas. If they ask about my interests and needs, it's a clear indication they're invested.

5. **Cancellation patterns speak volumes.** If someone cancels 2-3 times, it might be due to busyness, but often it indicates a lack of prioritization or desire to meet. If they cancel without proposing a new date, consider it a clear signal that things might be uphill from there. Use this as motivation to become even more compelling.

6. **Silence is telling.** If you leave a message, send a text, or email, and they don't return your call, take the hint. If you leave three or more messages, it's time to stop. They're likely not interested in continuing the conversation.

Are your relationships loyal?

Building strong, loyal relationships is crucial. You want people in your corner who not only support you but actively recommend you. When a relationship is loyal, you have an ambassador who will advocate for you; these are the allies you need. They serve as your eyes and ears in the field.

You know you have a loyal connection when they forgive minor missteps, recommend you to others, and take the time to provide constructive criticism. If they're willing to voice concerns and invest their energy in your growth, that's a sign of true loyalty.

Practice makes perfect

Many people think they're networking just because they attend conferences and engage in conversations with strangers. But when you ask them afterward whether they'd want to meet that person again to exchange ideas or explore business opportunities, the answer is often a hesitant "maybe."

Surprisingly, some individuals find that when they reach out to those they met, the person doesn't remember them or seems indifferent. This behavior can be perplexing, but to succeed at networking, it's essential to recognize that every relationship goes through stages before yielding real benefits. I'll delve into these phases in a later section.

The key to becoming a successful networker isn't just something you can read about; you need to get out there and practice. Experiment, celebrate your successes, and embrace your mistakes. Networking is a lifelong journey with no finish line. You will never reach a point where you can say, "I've mastered it."

Every person is unique, and that's why you must continually refine your social skills by pushing boundaries, embracing openness, and fostering tolerance.

How to get people to help you repeatedly

The key is to thank someone **three times** if you want them to help you again in the future.

If you only thank them once, they are likely to only help you that one time. But if you want people to continue helping, remember this: A great way to nurture relationships and encourage future help is to express your gratitude clearly and consistently - a total of three times.

Bad news? Saying "thank you" once, sending flowers, or giving a bottle of wine isn't enough. Over time, people who've helped you may start to feel you're ungrateful if you only thank them once - or worse, not at all. Unfortunately, most of us only express thanks one time, thinking that's enough. And let's be honest: thanking someone multiple times can feel a bit awkward or excessive.

But in my experience, developing a **"Thank-You Strategy"** is a game-changer.

The "3 Thank-Yous Strategy"

The idea is simple: **thank people three times.** Whenever someone helps you or takes time for you, your first thank-you should happen immediately after. But don't stop there - one thank-you isn't enough.

Let me give you a practical example. Say you land a job because someone in your network gave you a stellar recommendation. Of course, you should thank them right away! Most polite people do that much.

But what many don't do is follow up with more thanks. My advice? After you pass your probation period at the new job, get back in touch with the person who recommended you and say something like, "Thank you again for your recommendation - it really made a difference. I'm happy to share that I'll be staying with the company. Thanks again!"

That second thank-you reinforces your gratitude and reminds them that their help mattered. Then, let's say a year into the job, you reach out once more to let them know how things are going: "I just wanted to say thank you again. Things are going great, and I've achieved some exciting results. I'm truly grateful for your help."

At that point, your gratitude will feel so genuine that they'll have no doubt you appreciate their support. The natural response? They'll be more than willing to help you again if you need it. If you want continued support, one thank-you won't cut it - you need three!

Why you should thank even when the answer is no

It's important to show gratitude even when things don't go your way. For example, thank people who reject you. If someone takes the time to respond to your email, message, or phone call, that effort deserves a thank-you, regardless of the outcome.

Let me share a personal story. A young man once approached me after a talk I gave, asking if I would mentor him. I told him I couldn't - my schedule was too packed, and the timing wasn't right. He thanked me for spending five minutes talking with him anyway. A week later, he sent me an email to follow up, asking if I'd reconsider. Again, I politely declined and explained why. His response? Another thank-you - just for replying!

How often do you think I receive a thank-you after turning someone down? Almost never.

This young man was the first person to ever thank me for a rejection, and I respected him for it. I spend hours every month answering inquiries, and his persistence stood out. A few weeks later, he even sent me a book, with a note:

"Dear Soulaima, I know you're interested in strategy, as I am. Here's a book I believe is the best on the topic." I must admit, I was impressed by his thoughtfulness and determination. I noticed he had registered for another event I was speaking at, and you know what? I think I'll make time to chat with him!

Build a thank-you habit

Your thank-you strategy shouldn't be reserved only for big moments - it should apply to everyone:

- People who help you
- People who take time to respond to your emails, messages, or calls
- People who provide constructive feedback or advice

Use your calendar to track who you thanked, for what, and when. Set reminders for future thank-yous:

- **Thank you #1:** (Date)
- **Thank you #2:** (Date)
- **Thank you #3:** (Date)

But remember - don't thank someone more than three times. Anything beyond that, and you risk coming across as a bit... insincere.

Your IQ isn't everything

Do you consider yourself to be professionally skilled? Do you believe that guarantees your future? Unfortunately, that's merely your entry ticket. It's time to debunk the myth that you should solely focus on developing your technical skills. Your competencies and experiences quickly lose their uniqueness; news, knowledge, and innovations spread at the speed of the internet. This means you must cultivate a solid, loyal, and capable network to keep up with the times.

Skills and intelligence are worthless if you're not adept at staying updated, engaging with people, and communicating effectively.

From my experience, five qualities determine whether you reach your goals in life:

- Your ability to build trusting relationships
- Your capacity to brand yourself and showcase your core competencies
- Contributing your best while allowing others to do the same
- Helping others succeed
- Taking care of yourself to avoid burnout

Achieving this requires:

1. Energy
2. Passion
3. Integrity
4. Strategy

To elevate your networking game, embrace some key principles inspired by *the 48 Laws of Power* (one of my favorite books):

1. **Make others shine:** Focus on lifting those around you. When you help others succeed, you become an invaluable ally, building goodwill that pays off in the long run.

2. **Be discreet:** Keep your true intentions close to your chest. This allows you to connect without creating unnecessary competition. Genuine relationships often develop in the shadows.

3. **Cultivate a memorable presence:** While it's important not to overshadow others, you still want to be recognized for what makes you unique. Don't blend in - stand out for the right reasons.

4. **Stay connected:** Avoid isolating yourself. Engage actively with a diverse network to uncover fresh opportunities and insights.

5. **Embrace flexibility:** Don't rush into commitments. Stay open to various connections and possibilities; the best opportunities often come from unexpected places.

6. **Leverage shared values:** Find common ground that motivates those you want to connect with. Building on shared beliefs creates deeper bonds that are mutually beneficial.

By balancing your presence and fostering authentic relationships, you'll not only enhance your networking skills but also build a robust professional circle that propels you forward.

Are you an interesting conversationalist?

One of my superpowers is that I've interviewed hundreds of people - seriously, I've lost count! In fact, I've been at it weekly for my podcasts since 2017, which means I've racked up a staggering number of interviews. One thing I've learned. I can make even the most boring person feel incredibly interesting. It's like a magic trick! They open quickly, sharing personal stories that help me (and everyone else) get to know them in no time.

So, what's your superpower in conversations? Are you the "master of small talk," do you have a knack for uncovering hidden talents in people?

Anyway, to become a valuable resource for others, you must put in the effort to be someone people want to connect with. Reflect on your life, habits, and biases - have you switched to autopilot? Are you ready to challenge yourself to become a more attractive resource for others?

If so, here are some strategies to inspire you:

- Change jobs or seek a transfer for broader perspectives.
- Take on new tasks and responsibilities to gain fresh skills.
- Study something - anything nerdy - invest in yourself.
- Keep up with things!
- Move, repaint, or rearrange your living space; introduce vibrant, dynamic elements.
- Travel to new destinations, whether domestic or international.
- Challenge your biases by engaging with groups or individuals you might typically avoid.
- If you usually drive to work, take the bus or train instead.

- Initiate (small) conversations with at least two new people daily - at work, on the street, or on public transport.
- Watch different shows, read alternative news sources, listen to new music, and explore a new topic each week.
- Try new cuisines and visit different restaurants.

Many people successfully shake up their lives and shift their mindsets, remaining attractive networkers.

You can do the same if you choose to. By enhancing your ability to embrace change, you can transform a stagnant comfort zone into a thriving development zone, enhancing your capacity to network with diverse individuals who complement you.

Take a moment to assess where you stand in terms of the following qualities:

Quality	Low	Medium	High
Openness			
Tolerance			
Readiness for change			
Curiosity			

If you're ambitious about your own life, you need to keep up with the times and broaden your horizons. You must be able to embrace change and stay curious about what a new relationship or experience might bring.

This is particularly true in the business world. Companies are on the lookout for leaders and executives who can bring people together and navigate the complex, informal relationships within an organization.

Energy and passion: your currency

Think back to your last meeting, networking event, or conference. Who stands out in your memory? It's often not the person with the most impressive credentials but rather the individual who seamlessly blends expertise with personality. Passionate people radiate a unique energy that draws others in. When this energy is coupled with integrity and purpose, it creates a compelling mix that's hard to forget.

We don't encounter this combination often, but when we do, it leaves a lasting impression. Ask yourself: How do you present yourself in these interactions? Do people remember you after you part ways?

Most of us find ourselves in situations where our skills and talents remain largely unknown. To change this, strategic networking becomes essential. It's about transforming your relationships from unfamiliarity to genuine appreciation. As you engage with others, consider how your energy and vibrational presence influence their perception of you.

Remember, people are attracted to those who resonate with competence, positivity, and authenticity. Vibrance is your secret sauce. It's all about the magnetic presence you bring to conversations - think enthusiasm, passion, and a sprinkle of charisma. This is what makes people remember you long after you've left the room.

And then there's energy: your emotional and physical buzz. High energy can turn a dull chat into a lively exchange, drawing people in and making them eager to connect. So, if you want to elevate your networking game, lean into your vibrance and energy. They'll help you stand out and forge genuine connections that can open doors down the line.

Cultivating this not only enhances your networking but positions you as someone who is not just seen but truly valued in professional circles. Embrace your energy and watch how it transforms your interactions!

"Giving" is the new "taking"

To build a successful career, you need others in your corner. So, how do you ensure that more people recognize your skills and resources?

It all starts with projecting and communicating your passion for what you do best. Sounds simple, right? Unfortunately, it's not that easy. Many of us find ourselves in roles that don't align with our true strengths, often settling for whatever job comes our way. In fact, international studies show that about 80% of us aren't satisfied with our work lives, which can seriously hinder our ability to attract positive attention from others.

Additionally, we often struggle to articulate what we do and what makes us unique. We fall back on titles, job descriptions, or vague terms that don't really capture our skills and strengths. To make it easier for others to understand, support, and help you, focus on clarity and authenticity in your communication.

Share specific examples of your accomplishments and how they relate to your passions. When you simplify your message and make it relatable, you create a clear pathway for people to engage with you, making them more likely to want to support your journey. After all, when others can easily grasp your value, they're more inclined to champion you and your work.

I recommend starting with, "Hi, my name is _____, and I help people by [briefly describe what you do or the problems you solve]." This approach clearly communicates your value while inviting further conversation.

Not long ago, a young leader asked me, "What do you think is the best career path for me?" He was uncertain whether he was on the right track. I told him: "Ask yourself - what do you love doing so much that you'd still do it even if you weren't getting paid?"

That's where you'll find the key to what you should pursue.

Be authentic, be yourself, and stay true to what you love. Engage in work that genuinely interests you. Yet, many of us struggle to clearly articulate our biggest passions, and that's where the challenge lies. So, take the time to reflect on what truly excites you, and let that passion guide your career choices. When you align your work with your interests, you'll not only find fulfillment but also naturally attract the attention and support you need to thrive.

You have three networks

Your network typically divides into three key categories:

- **The personal** network
- **The expertise** network
- **The professional** network

The personal network

In your personal network, you know each other well - this often includes family and close friends. They play a crucial role when you need support, but they may not be the best source of help beyond emotional backing. A childhood friend, for instance, might hesitate to offer criticism, preferring to shield you from harsh truths. Family can sometimes be even less reliable as advisors; they may hold too much affection for you, be influenced by their own expectations, or be too affected by your version of events to provide honest, constructive feedback.

While your personal network is formed on shared beliefs and values, it isn't the optimal source of inspiration. Your mentors and inspirations should be chosen based on their strengths, knowledge, and skills.

In my experience, it's often acquaintances - not family - who propel my professional growth and refer me for business opportunities. Few people will advocate for you to their boss, and most workplaces prefer to avoid hiring candidates with family ties. A recommendation and an opened door from an acquaintance can carry far more weight. Acquaintances find it easier to leverage connections for contacts and contracts.

The expertise network

Most of us lack a clear understanding of who we know within our Expertise networks - how well we know them, the strength of our relationships, their core competencies, and their professional needs and goals. The Expertise Network is distinct from your personal network, which typically includes family and close friends who are familiar with your private life.

Your Expertise Network consists of those with whom you share specialized knowledge or professional insights, often connected by shared education, industry, or field of expertise. You may work in the same department or company or belong to professional groups focused on specific areas of expertise. Typically, we engage most deeply with those we collaborate with and feel a sense of professional camaraderie.

To determine whether you're investing your time wisely within your Expertise Network, start by reviewing your company's organizational chart. Mark the names of the individuals you have professional relationships with. Then, place a green check next to those with whom you share a strong, mutually beneficial connection. For those who aren't marked yet, divide them into two groups: those who aren't critical (mark with yellow) and those with whom you should work on developing a stronger connection (mark with red).

Now, you have a clearer picture of who you know well within your Expertise Network and where there are gaps. From here, create an action plan to nurture or expand relationships with those marked in red, ensuring your network is both valuable and well-rounded.

Networking for Underdogs

Suggested actions (complete the list yourself):

- Invite the person to a meeting and discuss how you can mutually benefit from each other.
- Change seats in the cafeteria to meet people other than those you usually sit with.
- Participate in events organized by your company or your professional association.
- _____
- _____
- _____

Map your expertise network:

Who do you mostly talk to at work? Writer their names in the circle.

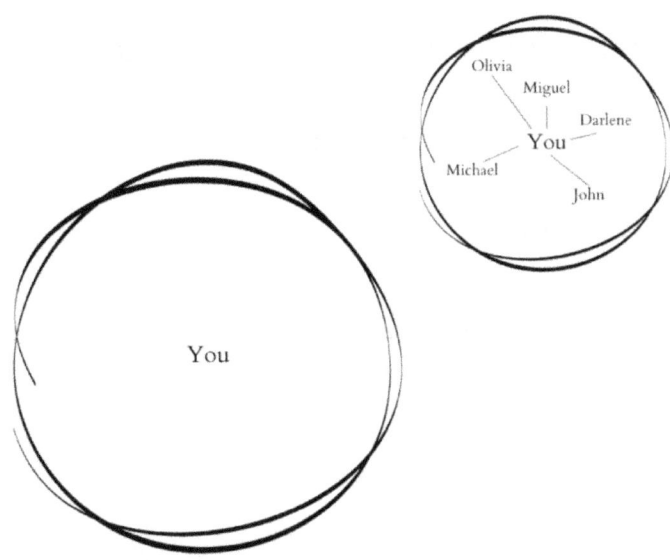

The professional network

The professional network consists of people from various sectors of the business world.

Ideally, they do not have the same professional expertise as you but represent different industries and areas of competence from which you can learn. You typically meet them at conferences, trade shows, business dinners, business trips, and other places where people are independent of industry, job position, etc.

In the professional network, you are personal but not private with your relationships. Specifically, this means you build a level of trust with your business contacts. Trust is established when you share a bit of yourself. However, if you share too much with your connections, they may gain knowledge that they would rather not have. It's a fine balance.

Most people's networks typically consist of:

80% personal relationships

15% expertise relationships

5% professional relationships

Who makes up your professional network?

Consider who your most important professional relationships are. Think about former clients or, for example, collaborators.

Name:
Name:
Name:
Name:
Name:
Name:

Did you identify many or few? How strong is your relationship with each of these? Try to mark where you believe your relationship stands.

It's important to think about how you can develop these relationships. Consider concrete ways to strengthen your connection with each person, so they all move into the medium or strong range.

The 3 magical circles

To create a complete overview, I recommend that you view your network as three circles.

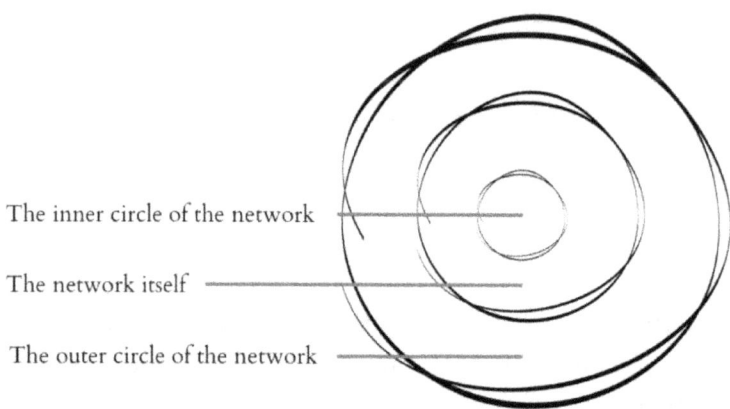

The inner circle of the network

The network itself

The outer circle of the network

The inner circle:

Your inner circle consists of the most important people in your life, both professionally and personally. They should be more skilled and influential than you, fully supporting your goals 100%. Write down the names of those who are crucial for you to achieve your career aspirations. Typically, your inner circle will consist of about 10 to 12 individuals. What do you know about them? Are you aware of their key needs and dreams? Selecting the people in your inner circle requires careful consideration.

When you include someone in your inner circle, you're committing to invest over 60% of your networking time with them. This circle may include your mentor, if you have one. Think of your inner circle as a small board of advisors, complementing your life and career. Your personal network doesn't belong here. Moreover, there should be no individuals in your inner circle that you don't already know. However, you can certainly have a plan for who you wish to add to your inner circle in the long run. This means actively recruiting them and nurturing those relationships so that one day they become some of the most important people in your network.

Name	The person's most important needs right now.	The person's wishes for the future.

It's crucial that they understand your aspirations for the future and your most pressing needs right now. You don't necessarily have to be one of their top priorities. Their inclusion in your inner circle doesn't have to be reciprocated. Typically, when you choose an inner circle of individuals who are significantly more skilled than you, you may find yourself in a junior position in their eyes. That's perfectly fine, if they genuinely have a positive attitude and take an interest in your success.

Your inner circle evolves continuously as you grow. This means your needs may shift, and so might the people you require in your innermost network.

Your network:

The people in your broader network aren't as familiar to you as those in your inner circle. They know who you are but not in the same depth. Typically, your network may consist of around 50 individuals. These relationships are essential and may include potential candidates for your inner circle. This group encompasses everyone who falls under the category of "acquaintances." These are the individuals you can call who recognize your name and would be willing to return your call if you reach out.

The Outer Circle:

The outer circle comprises a vast number of people you don't know well. Here, you might have several hundred contacts - everyone you encounter in your daily life. You may only know someone's first name, and typically, you don't have much knowledge about everyone. Mapping out your outer circle can be insightful as it serves as an inspiration list for whom you might recruit for further dialogue and develop relationships with.

You can map your outer circle by reviewing your life chronologically. Consider your old friends, sports clubs, classmates, your child's network, former colleagues, past clients, and schoolmates. Look through address books, business card holders, contact lists, old emails, Facebook, LinkedIn, and any other platforms where you have contacts recorded.

Gather this information in one place so you have a clear overview of your outer circle. Some prefer to start here and later categorize the names into the inner circles. Reflect on whether there are individuals in your network you'd like to move closer to, whom you wish to know better, or conversely, those you may want to distance yourself from. Ensure you maintain your data, lists, and information securely to avoid losing them. Most people store their lists and contacts on their computers and phones. Consider how you can protect this data. Common situations where hard work and meticulous records can be lost include:

- Losing your computer (e.g., during a job loss)
- Losing access to your email system and address lists
- Fire
- Theft
- System failure

Nurturing Your Network:

Networking is about providing value before asking for anything or seeking favors from your connections. You should consider how best to nurture your network, evaluating your resources, including time, money, willingness, and energy. Offer your connections experiences, time, knowledge, or simply your company.

Consider the following for each or the circles:

The inner circle:

- Who do I want to develop a deeper relationship with and nurture thoroughly?
- How many hours per month can I allocate to maintain direct contact with these individuals?

The network:

- Who and how will I nurture this group?

The outer circle:

- Who and how will I nurture this group?

How to integrate networking into your busy daily life!

- Be more proactive internally and externally?
- Send three proactive emails each week?
- Make two proactive phone calls each week?

- Arrange a lunch meeting each week?
- Join a networking group once a month?

Meaningful over expensive

Once you've identified the key individuals in your network, it's time to nurture your connections with them.

Try to discover if they have any needs you can assist with. Active participation in your network is essential, and it's vital to care for your relationships thoughtfully. Remember that everyone requires different forms of nurturing.

Relationships should no longer rely on expensive dinners, luxury car rides, or lavish trips. While you can still host VIP events for your most significant connections, their nature has shifted. Instead, involve your connections in "meaningful" causes and initiatives. Consider swapping the usual lunch for something more impactful, like joining a community cleanup at a local beach or in a neighborhood.

Offer them an experience! Give people something that enriches them - mentally, of course. Individuals who link their relationships to positive, memorable experiences tend to forge stronger connections than those who only meet for coffee or in sterile meeting rooms. It's crucial that the experiences you invite them to are:

- Authentic (they should resonate with you).
- Community-driven.
- Inviting of engagement.

There are significant differences in how various generations within your network prefer to be nurtured. Some may favor establishing and maintaining contact through regular in-person meetings, while others might prefer a blend of physical gatherings and virtual networking. Some individuals quickly build trust, while others need more time to develop those connections.

Here's an overview of the different generations and their typical preferences for nurturing:

Connection type	Baby boomers	Gen X	Gen Y	Gen Z
In-person	To great extent	In the beginning	To little extent	Not at all
Email/letter	To great extent	To great extent	To little extent	Not at all
Call/text	No text	To great extent	To great extent	Texts
Social media	To little extent	To some extent	To great extent	To greatest extent
Trips/gifts	To great extent	To some extent	To some extent	To little extent

Across all generations, there is a growing emphasis on value-based networking, where relationships are built on shared purpose rather than mere transactions.

By adapting networking strategies to accommodate these diverse preferences - combining face-to-face meetings with digital tools and fostering inclusive, value-driven interactions - professionals can cultivate stronger connections and more effective relationships.

Expand your network

You may find yourself in a situation, or will soon, where your network needs to be updated with new profiles and new skills. In this context, it's essential to consider where you can meet those you are missing. Who or what skills do you lack in your network? Can you be specific?

If your current network cannot help you achieve your goals, you need to go out and "recruit." Identify the skills or specific individuals you need in your network, and then use your existing network to find out if you know anyone who knows someone who knows the person. If that doesn't yield results, find out where else you can meet these people. Allow your relationships to represent a different age, industry, and educational background than your own. This will enhance your approach to problem-solving.

Describe the skills or specific individuals you lack to fulfill your professional, career, and personal goals. Start by outlining the skills you do not possess but find necessary to achieve your goal:

1.
2.
3.
4.
5.

Next, focus on finding out where you can meet people who have the skills you seek. Try writing down the names of people you have heard about, read about, or spoken with whom you would like to build a relationship:

Person's name:
Person's name:
Person's name:

Actively reach out to people through your existing network, emails, direct phone calls, and social media platforms like LinkedIn, Facebook, Twitter, as well as specific conferences where you can find the right individuals. Tell the people you meet that you dream of meeting this or that person. Ask them for good advice on how to contact the right ones or if they know someone you should reach out to. You will be surprised at how willing people are to help you.

The 20-minute rule: small habits, big impact

Throughout my life, I've made it a mission to help others - whether it's landing a job, securing funding, making the right introduction, or simply being there at a pivotal moment. It's never been about keeping score or seeking recognition; it's just how I choose to live.

And it's not just because I've been helped along the way - it's because I believe that lifting others up is one of the most meaningful things we can do.

The power of 20 minutes

One practice that has profoundly shaped my journey is something I call the 20-Minute Rule. Every day, I dedicate 20 minutes - sometimes more, but never less - to making a difference. In those minutes, I might:

- Make a phone call, a WhatsApp message - you name it - to offer encouragement
- Send an email introduction
- Share advice
- Open a door for someone seeking an opportunity

It may not sound like much, but 20 minutes a day adds up in powerful ways. Even on the busiest days, carving out this time is possible - and it's a small investment with a massive return.

The ripple effect of small acts

A few weeks ago, I was reminded of just how impactful these small moments can be. I found myself in a room full of friends and fellow leaders from the World Economic Forum's Young Global Leaders (YGL) community. During the gathering, they were asked to stand if I had influenced their lives in any way - whether I had made a call, given advice, or offered support, not just once but multiple times over the years.

To my surprise, no one sat down. Not after 10, 20, or even 400 acts of help. Everyone remained standing.

In that moment, I was overcome with emotion. What started as small, seemingly insignificant actions had blossomed into something far greater than I ever imagined. The seeds of kindness I had sown - phone calls, introductions, small favors - had grown into a profound and visible impact.

Why it matters

The experience hit me hard and served as a powerful reminder: the ripple effect of our actions is often greater than we can comprehend. A simple introduction or a few kind words can change the course of someone's life in ways we'll never fully understand.

This is why I encourage you to embrace the 20-Minute Rule - commit to spending just a small part of your day helping others. Open a door, share advice, or extend a hand. It's not about grand gestures; it's about consistency.

These small acts don't just make a difference in someone else's life - they also shape the legacy we leave behind. Our impact on others is, in the end, the truest measure of our success.

Start today

So, here's my challenge: Start today. Commit to 20 minutes a day to help someone - whether it's sending a supportive message, making an introduction, or giving advice. It may feel like a small effort now, but over time, it becomes a force for good.

Let's create ripples that travel farther than we can imagine. The legacy we leave behind is built moment by moment, interaction by interaction. And I, for one, am committed to making mine count.

When you are facing the person; as a rule of thumb, you should always aim to know the following about a person:

- The professional aspect
- The personal aspect
- The future (the person in 1-3 years)

To get to know the person better, you should prepare some questions you want to ask.

Write down which questions you want to ask.

1. _____
2. _____
3. _____
4. _____

Feel free to repeat this exercise with your closest advisors. For 1-2 minutes, try to steer the conversation so that both you and the person you're speaking with can share as much relevant information as possible.

INSPIRATION

- *What do you do when you're not working?*
- *What do you like to read?*
- *What challenges are you facing in your work right now?*
- *How can I or others help you right now?*
- *What do you consider to be your greatest success so far?*

Essential qualities of a networker

- Present yourself positively.
- Avoid speaking poorly of others, even when tempted; keep your inner critic in check.
- Allow others to share their thoughts.
- Ask insightful questions.

When networking, you often find yourself in a conversation with others. It's crucial to give them space to express what matters while making the most of the limited time you have. Being a good networker means taking responsibility not only for your career but also for the careers of those around you. You have a duty to assist when two or more factors are present:

1. You have the time.
2. You possess the necessary skills.
3. You know someone who can help.

A networking conversation is a dialogue - a dynamic exchange of words and body language between two or more individuals seeking to establish a relationship. In this exchange, each participant takes turns being the sender or receiver. The art of networking lies in sustaining a conversation with a stranger that goes beyond small talk, enabling you to learn enough about the person to discern how you can assist them, and vice versa. This interaction is not merely about exchanging information; it's about building and maintaining meaningful relationships.

As a guideline, a conversation where both parties get to speak should last between 45 minutes and 1 to 2 hours. While it's possible to shorten it to about 30 minutes, most of us need more time to truly understand another person.

The anatomy of a good networking conversation

- Both parties get a chance to speak.
- There's a balanced exchange of questions and answers.
- You ensure your conversation partner understands your current and future needs so they can provide the necessary support.
- The conversation aims for genuine clarity or mutual understanding.
- Confidentiality is maintained throughout.

The 70/30 rule

This simple principle suggests that during 70% of your time together, it's appropriate to discuss professional topics - tasks, challenges, and other work-related matters. The remaining 30% should be dedicated to personal topics (not private ones). Talk about what's on your mind - interests, concerns, joys. Similarly, inquire about these aspects with your conversation partner. Pay attention to the small, personal stories they share and follow up on them the next time you meet. Share a bit of yourself to foster an informal and personal connection.

What are your core competencies?

When networking, it's vital that you can succinctly introduce yourself so that the person you're speaking with quickly understands your needs. Articulating your competencies and goals can be challenging, but it's essential for maximizing the value of a networking conversation.

People want to know what you can offer so they can identify how they can utilize your skills. Be specific when presenting yourself to others. In many situations, you'll find yourself speaking with someone unfamiliar with your background. How will you ensure that, after the conversation, they remember you and your competencies?

You are undoubtedly skilled in many areas, but what are you most proficient at? What do you excel in? It's possible that you find what you can do to be trivial. If so, ask someone in your network what they believe your strongest skills are.

If I were in your shoes, I would reach out to the five most constructively critical people I know and ask them directly, "What do you think my core competencies are?" This knowledge is crucial because their feedback may reveal why you do or do not have the network you aspire to.

You should aim to craft a 10-second networking profile that includes:

- Your name
- The name of your company/department
- A brief overview of what you do, emphasizing the needs you fulfill/the value you add rather than the tasks/job you perform
- A statement about how you help people

Networking without a job

In my work with the long-term unemployed, the first thing people talk about is shame - how they've lost their spark, their self-respect, and their sense of dignity.

And this cuts across professions: I've heard it from waiters, cleaners, teachers, bankers, and academics alike. It's nearly impossible to build a future when you feel this way, which is why restoring that sense of self-worth must come first.

Often, we struggle to get the help we need because we're not clear about what we're asking for - or how we can contribute in return. To make it easier for others to help or connect with you, focus on being specific and intentional.

The key is to know yourself well - understand your needs, strengths, and what you bring to the table. Communicate clearly so others can quickly understand who you are and how they can support you.

Respect yourself, stay open, and be of service to others. When you approach relationships with both self-awareness and generosity, they often lead to meaningful directions you couldn't have planned for.

Your value as a human isn't determined by what you've achieved, how much you've earned, or the title you hold.

It's something deeper, and reclaiming that understanding is the foundation for any meaningful progress.

Networking when you're between jobs, a stay-at-home spouse, or in transition can feel awkward - so how do you engage without a job to reference? The key is to focus not on what you do, but how you're spending your time and the value you bring to those around you. Life isn't just about work; it's about impact.

Talk about the contributions you make to your community, the projects you've tackled, and the skills you've honed along the way. Your competencies and experiences are still valid currency, regardless of where you are in your career.

If you don't know precisely what you're looking for, that's not a limitation - it's an opportunity. Stay open to what might unfold. Conversations spark ideas, and ideas often lead to opportunities you didn't see coming. A title or formal role isn't what makes a connection valuable - your perspective and potential do.

Don't let the absence of a position define your networking efforts. Build relationships intentionally, and you'll discover that networks built on shared value are the ones that thrive long-term.

As you step into the world, let your networking efforts be guided by empathy and kindness. Seek to understand those around you and listen actively. Celebrate the diversity of experiences and perspectives that enrich our networks.

Together, we can create powerful ecosystems where everyone can thrive. Let us harness the power, wisdom, joy, and wealth that come from genuine connections. Grow, learn, and pass it on. As you move forward, I encourage you to connect with intention, embrace the stories of others, and remember that the true power of networking lies in the quality of the relationships we build.

Let us aspire to create networks that not only elevate our careers but also foster a sense of community and belonging. Together, we can shape a brighter, more interconnected future.

The 9 networking types and personalities

Read through the following 9 networking types and consider which type you are. All 9 types have strengths and weaknesses, and it's incredibly important to know these to get the most out of networking. With this as the final section in the book, you should now be able to go out and network strategically and optimally.

Network type 1: "The responsible networker"

You perceive yourself as a responsible and good person. You are dutiful, with a strong sense of ethics and morals. You tend to be quite hard on yourself and often take on more responsibility than you should.

We live in what is called a network society, which means that we all depend on relationships to achieve our individual and organizational goals.

Your ability to build trustworthy relationships, which are loyal to you, is essential for gaining access to contacts, contracts, inspiration, influence, and information.

In short, the defining characteristic of this era is that, unlike in previous periods, you can no longer reasonably expect to fully oversee all aspects of your job, as the world has become so complex, and the contexts you are a part of are increasingly abstract and diffuse. We are in a phase with a focus on a "new" kind of capitalism, often referred to as knowledge capitalism.

Characteristics of the type 1 networker

This development presents a particular challenge for you as a Type 1 networker, as you prefer to handle all your tasks through your own skills and efforts. You are used to being accountable for the work you do, and you take pride in meeting your deadlines and performing your work with professional integrity.

The challenge for you will be to accept living in a time where knowledge is constantly changing, and where you often rely on the competencies of others to keep up with the demands of the time.

There are nine different networking archetypes. Your archetype represents your primary networking identity. Your network type identifies your attitudes, beliefs, and social behavior in networking situations.

Networking is divided into three disciplines:

- Mapping network relationships
- Maintaining existing professional and business relationships

- Expanding your network to include future and new professional and business relationships

Considering your thorough approach to handling your responsibilities, it will often be an advantage for the Type 1 networker to have few, but close, network relationships. Your general approach to fulfilling your responsibilities means that you prefer to do things properly. This likely applies to your network as well. You may become frustrated if you have so many relationships to maintain that it prevents you from being fully present. Therefore, it is crucial for the Type 1 networker to conduct a thorough mapping of their network, ensuring that you have a clear overview of who is relevant for you to invest your energy in.

Network type 2: "The giving networker"

Your self-perception is that you are caring, considerate, empathetic, "a good friend," responsible, and engaged.

Most jobs are filled through networking. There is disagreement about the exact percentage, but it is certain that it is well over half of all jobs. Recent studies suggest that the likelihood of landing your dream job is up to ten times higher if the job is found through networking rather than through traditional job searching.

You either take advantage of this, or you must rely on the standard procedure for job searching. There is no doubt that traditional job searching can be tempting, as it merely requires you to create a CV and an application and send them to the company. Finding a job through networking, however, demands much more from you and places significant requirements on your ability to create and maintain relationships that are mutual, loyal, and strategic. You need to get out and meet people and talk to relevant individuals within your current and future networks.

Characteristics of the type 2 networker

To become truly skilled at networking, you must spend time understanding your strengths and using them. As a Type 2 networker, you have many admirable and sympathetic qualities, but like anyone else, they can become obstacles when you need to interact with new, unfamiliar people who do not yet know you.

You are a typical Type 2 networker if you feel the need to be needed and appreciated. Others are naturally inclined to network with you because you are so good at helping others. People love individuals who can and are willing to help.

You thrive on being valuable to your relationships and feel genuinely happy when they need your help. This is undoubtedly positive, but your challenge is to remember both to give and to take. Especially to take, so that you also gain something from the relationship.

To build a mutually strong and loyal relationship, you must remember to take (i.e., ensure that your own needs are met). A relationship becomes stronger when both parties feel they are benefitting.

You will typically fall into one of two categories. First, as "The Neutral Opener," where you talk about neutral topics while you circle around the food or wait to greet the host.

You often rely on safe situations (the food table, gift table, restroom line, congratulatory queue, etc.). You primarily discuss neutral topics with those you happen to stand next to, sit next to, or already know. You are generally polite and may come across as slightly distant. You feel relieved when you meet someone you know because you can then stand comfortably with them—safe and secure. You position yourself where you won't attract too much attention.

Alternatively, you could be "The Follower." Many of us, in fact, become followers when we find ourselves in gatherings with many people, where we must integrate and find our place.

The crucial thing for a follower is not to stand out from the crowd or draw too much attention. You discreetly blend into the conversation that others are having. In other words, you quietly join the group. You position yourself where the others are.

Do you find it difficult to ask others for help? One thing that holds many Type 2s back from asking for help is the fact that power dynamics come into play. When you ask for help, you elevate the helper to a higher position than yourself, automatically granting them power. For a Type 2 networker, this may be the reason why you hesitate to ask for help, as it makes you feel vulnerable.

Personally, I have had many positive experiences asking for help. It is up to you to ensure that, when you find yourself in situations where you lack the necessary skills and experience, you ask for help from those you believe are more skilled and experienced than yourself.

Network type 3: "The persistent networker"

Your self-perception is that you are goal-oriented, persistent, a self-starter, pragmatic, and good at adapting and completing your projects.

Characteristics of the type 3 networker

You are undoubtedly perceived as a determined and strong individual; someone people trust and believe will achieve the goals you set for yourself. You naturally attract people who admire your steadfastness and drive to reach the top (or whatever you are striving for).

If you are a Type 3 networker, you may be the kind of person who needs to feel that others appreciate, admire, and look up to you to feel successful.

You might recognize yourself in this: you often take on the role of "the successful one," and you're someone who is perceived as living "the happy life" (whatever that means!). This can be difficult to live up to all the time, and it likely takes a lot of energy from you.

In a successful networking relationship, the key dynamic between two people is trust. Therefore, it's not always advisable to present a perfect image of yourself. No one lives an entirely flawless life, and people feel uneasy if you don't show your humanity.

When you're stressed or under pressure, others may perceive you as conflicted or secretive. But when you're on top of things, you come across as attractive, authentic, eloquent, and humble.

People remember you if you inspire trust. Individuals are drawn to those who remind them of something familiar from other (comfortable) situations. As the well-known psychologist Robert Zajonc points out, we are inclined to choose those we feel secure with. He emphasizes that we like what we remember. Do people remember you when they've met you? And do they remember you for something positive? It's important that people remember you for something good and for something they have a high degree of personal and professional trust in.

Your personality must evoke trust - otherwise, of course, people won't place their trust in you. People have become more critical, and they are looking for authentic, meaningful, and trustworthy relationships, something or someone they can rely on - especially if they are considering hiring you for a new job. Trust is a crucial factor for building a successful career, but it is also the hardest thing to create and the easiest thing to lose.

In other words, your market value is created through your positive energy and your ability to build emotional connections. However, to succeed in this, you must be authentic.

Network type 4: "The proud networker"

Your self-perception is that you are emotional in a good way, sensitive, focused on inner worlds, different, unique, and creative.

Characteristics of the type 4 networker

You are constantly challenged to combine your ability to act as a specialist, when necessary, while also thinking broadly like a generalist. Like many others, you are continuously pressured to be adaptable to change. No matter what your network type is, you can bring your qualities into play if you have a genuine interest in others. Your ability to be curious and engaged is a key competence in your interactions with others.

Many of us experience the expectation to research (rather than rely on ready knowledge) and solve problems in new ways to avoid reproducing old, familiar knowledge. Very few of us work in isolation. Therefore, it is important that you and your colleagues can deliver as a group, get people to collaborate, and share knowledge.

In a world with increasingly flat hierarchies, it is crucial that you can motivate others to take responsibility and make highly qualified decisions quickly. This is where you, as a Type 4, excel (when you are happy and in harmony). You possess an innate strength as a networker, which is highly valued in the business world.

Your desire to help others achieve success and victory is your greatest contribution, both to yourself and to others. Your intentions are reflected in your ability and willingness to map, nurture, and expand your relationships - and when you help others succeed.

You become stronger when you are skilled at networking because you can draw complementary knowledge from your network when you find yourself in situations where you lack experience, tools, or contacts to solve professional challenges. In other words, as a Type 4, you can draw substantial help from your network, allowing you to remain adaptable to change.

As a Type 4, you often see other values in networking, because you experience doing something good for yourself, something good for others, and contributing to the community. You will likely find that this enhances your ability to be goal-oriented, creative, and productive.

You meet people in many different situations, and like the other types, you should be aware of how to optimize each interaction, getting the most out of every meeting and dialogue. This helps you build, nurture, and expand your professional and business network. Additionally, you must be aware of how you come across to others.

When you are in your element and in a good state of balance, people perceive you as a very present, original person, and you are seen as warm and charming, with a great understanding and insight into others. This is highly attractive.

Network type 5: "The rational networker"

Your self-perception is that you are insightful, quick-witted, "sharp," curious, playful, alert, and unusual.

We know that people who network have easier access to inspiration, information, and influence - both in and out of the workplace. Type 5 believes they can do it all themselves. But the question is, does a Type 5 need to know everything on their own?

We live in a society saturated with information and a high demand for knowledge. The concept of knowledge is intangible, and it is difficult for others - and even for you - to determine whether you are the most skilled, best, or most competent. Knowledge is far too complex for that. In essence, the knowledge society is characterized by the fact that knowledge has gained far greater significance for individual success, corporate competitiveness, and national prosperity than ever before.

Knowledge is the most important tool for managing the increasing complexity and rapid changes that define our society.

Characteristics of a type 5 networker

Type 5 perceives knowledge as the only commodity. To a certain extent, that is true.

Knowledge has always been and will remain a sought-after asset. More and more companies are producing and trading in knowledge rather than physical goods, but your knowledge only has value if it is shared, or if the people who need to know it, know it. Your knowledge has an uncertain shelf life. Neither you nor I can predict when your knowledge will become obsolete (but it will!).

In contrast, you know when you can expect your computer to stop working, how long a vacuum cleaner will last, or when a particular amount of raw material will be depleted. It's much more difficult with knowledge, which is a scarce and perishable substance. You should critically assess when to upgrade yourself, and from whom you gather knowledge and inspiration. All information is available to those who search long and hard enough. Your access to knowledge is not the point; the key is how you package and use your knowledge.

You should ask yourself if you are sharing your knowledge sufficiently. Knowledge spreads more easily than other goods, especially in these times when people are more active on social media and online forums than ever before.

If you are a typical Type 5, you tend to keep your knowledge to yourself, and today this will challenge you, as it is difficult to prevent others - besides your customer, boss, or colleague - from accessing it.

You should not fear that your knowledge will spread; it increases your market value. What good is it if, for example, you are the world's best coder, but no one knows it?

If you refuse to share your knowledge, be aware that people will be less inclined to share their knowledge with you, and over time, you may become significantly less informed and enlightened than those who generously share their valuable knowledge. If your knowledge is difficult to spread, it will also be difficult to sell. If your knowledge remains hidden, it becomes tacit knowledge.

You live in a society overwhelmed by too much information, too little concrete knowledge, rapid changes, and sudden needs and challenges. Particularly if you work in the financial sector (e.g., as an advisor with client contact), you will experience a growing demand to build and maintain relationships (e.g., with clients, so they develop a strong, loyal, trusting connection with you and the company).

When you have built a strong network of competent people who excel in areas where you lack expertise, then - by leveraging your entire network - you represent a much larger knowledge base than you would on your own, and this benefits your clients and colleagues. As a Type 5, this means you don't need to know everything yourself, allowing you to step back and enjoy life beyond books, newspapers, and so on.

As a Type 5, you have a need to find the manual. It doesn't exist!

Networking is a lifelong process with no finish line. You will never be "good enough" at it.

Everyone is different, and since you need to network with many different types of people, you must continually develop yourself as a networker. You must constantly evolve:

- Your social skills
- Your attitude towards others
- Your comfort zone

People are different and must be treated accordingly. There are guidelines and good advice, but no actual manual.

Type 5 is typically a specialist, and like many specialists, you may believe that the world is rational and that there is a logical explanation for why people network with whom. But that's just not how it works.

Social and cultural events affect us all. The experiences of other types besides yourself shape their behavior, attitudes, prejudices, and beliefs. The more diverse types you have in your network, the greater your understanding of others, and the more diversity you will have access to.

As mentioned at the beginning, you rely on knowledge and access to a knowledge and competence pool to succeed, and your network is, in many ways, a web you can activate to ensure both your career and the careers of others. Your network is the optimal way to remain attractive in the job market. Will a boss want to hire someone who works solo as an old-fashioned specialist? Or will they prefer someone who, in a relatively short time, can allocate over 250 unique competencies depending on the challenge the employee is facing? The answer seems obvious.

Network type 6: "The skeptical networker"

Your self-perception is that you are reliable, trustworthy, thorough, sensible, cautious, and foresighted.

You possess strong qualities that are particularly useful when it comes to building strategic relationships with others. However, your challenge may be your strong need to have control over the situation, the framework, and the people you surround yourself with.

Regardless of your type, you can put your qualities to good use if you have a genuine interest in the tasks ahead. Your ability to be curious and engaged is a key competence when learning to network more effectively in the pursuit of a new or better job.

Here is a brief description of your personality type, which you can use for fun, to gain a better understanding of yourself, or to tailor your efforts in the pursuit of your dream job.

Characteristics of a type 6 networker

What Type 6 needs to remember is that networking is a way of thinking and working - it's an activity.

All your current and potential relationships should be categorized so that you have a clear overview of who you know, how well you know them, and how loyal your mutual relationships are. This is known as strategic networking.

The discipline of networking involves mapping who you know, nurturing those you know, and expanding with those you don't yet know but need to.

You are naturally well-suited to have this structure under control. However, sometimes you need to let go and allow yourself to be surprised, especially when it comes to people. Relationships evolve, and some come and go. Some people can be trusted, and others cannot. That's the lesson of life. Relationships don't need to last forever.

A network is like an herb garden, where you sow, water, and eventually harvest. By this, I mean that you need to build and nurture your relationships before you need them. If you think it sounds time-consuming to maintain a relationship, you're right. That's why I don't recommend networking with more people than you can reasonably maintain - especially for someone like Type 6, given your strong sense of loyalty.

A relationship must be nurtured and developed continuously; otherwise, it loses its value.

All relationships have a life cycle - some last a lifetime, while others last only a few weeks. The important thing is to be aware that a relationship develops over time.

As time passes, you will feel a greater sense of connection and trust, and eventually, the relationship becomes informal as you both feel more secure in each other's company.

Whether or not you move through all the phases depends on your ability and willingness to develop a relationship from unknown to familiar.

Most of us are best at establishing relationships, but few are skilled at optimizing and developing them. Many people are good at opening doors and getting contact details, but turning a relationship into something informal and mutually meaningful is an art.

Take your time to get to know a relationship, so you can give each person individual treatment that aligns with their expectations.

Perhaps you are an introverted Type 6?

It is often said that extroverts have an easier time succeeding through others. In my view, it's not that simple. Introverts have clear advantages when it comes to networking. They are extremely good at one-on-one relationships and often develop deeper connections. This happens less frequently for extroverts.

In fact, many extroverts are actually shy. It's a taboo, but it's common - even among leaders. They hide it as best they can. If you are shy around other people, that shyness can eventually lead to isolation in the organization and a reluctance to represent the company at receptions and events.

Do you know if you are approachable and sociable? Do people find you easy to be around? Do they find you easy to contact? Do people like you the first time they meet you? It's important for you to know how others perceive you, so you can ensure you are the best version of yourself.

When you are at your best and in balance, as a Type 6, you will be expressive, fearless, persistent, and loyal. You will come across as trustworthy, deliver quality work, be meticulous, and good at persuading others in a well-meaning way.

The idea that your (good) mood, (positive) energy level, and ability to be interesting and interested in others directly affect people's ability to remember you, do business with you, and recommend you (for example, to a new job) is supported by numerous studies, including those from The Academy of Management Journal. They map and prove that your mood and energy level directly influence people's willingness to recommend you to others (such as a potential new employer).

Network type 7: "The adventurous networker"

Your self-perception is that you are enthusiastic, a free spirit, spontaneous, cheerful, eager, outgoing, adventurous, and energetic.

As a Type 7 networker, you can be quite captivating to others, often becoming the center of attention because you enjoy being lively and fun. As a typical Type 7, you like to get to the point quickly, so here are the main points as fast as possible (otherwise, you might not keep reading!).

Characteristics of a type 7 networker

A Type 7 who is at their best is a content person who appears cheerful, full of energy, vibrant, ecstatic, and grateful.

If you are a Type 7 and are in your so-called generous space, you will come across as non-judgmental and highly tolerant of others' opinions and ideas.

A Type 7 inspires others with their zest for life and an insatiable appetite for laughter and experiences. So, if you are a Type 7, you may seem carefree and easygoing.

However, when stressed or out of balance, you can come across as childish, unpredictable, irresponsible, and may even appear slightly bitter or melancholic. Your communication can become sharp and sarcastic.

When you're among others, you seem like someone who enjoys meeting new people and don't focus much on those you already know. You generally do well in large gatherings, which is a positive trait.

However, you should be mindful of not appearing shallow. It's important that you show that you *do* have depth.

When it comes to relationships, your high energy and need for adventure and variety can lead you to rush ahead rather than taking the time to develop a relationship. You may come across as someone who struggles to focus on one person and your conversation. This is unfortunate, as you miss out on the depth that comes from having a solid network. Loose connections without mutual engagement don't create the same value.

Your network is your only guaranteed path to competence development. You can pursue as much education as you like, but nothing compares to a loyal, competent network - it offers concentrated knowledge and is the direct path to individual and organizational success. Even though you are a very smart and competent Type 7, your knowledge, too, has an uncertain shelf life.

Network type 8: "The action-oriented networker"

Your self-perception is that you are strong, confident, full of ideas, action-oriented, direct, tenacious, and resilient. You believe you have the right to say what you want, when you want.

You have a magnetic energy that captivates others. You're the kind of person people remember if they've met you, which is a big advantage when it comes to networking. Being memorable is the first step to building a relationship.

Your biggest challenge is that you expend so much energy being around others that you may feel drained after a business dinner, a training session, or a conference. You give a lot of energy to others. When you are at your best - recharged, in a good mood, and ready - you come across as strong, inspiring, brave, and fair. People turn to you because you are stable and can support and encourage others by speaking both directly and thoughtfully.

Characteristics of a type 8 networker

You have a natural talent for:

- Integrity
- Responsibility
- Passion
- Energy

You often come across as grounded and present, while also demonstrating a great deal of empathy for others - you are aware of the consequences of your actions and demeanor. People tend to have strong opinions about you - either they like you, or they don't. In other words, you polarize.

If I were you, I would call the five most constructive, critical people you know and ask them directly, "How do I come across to people in various situations?" This feedback is important because it may reveal the reasons you do or don't have the dream job or network you desire.

Try taking the test below. You need to mark where you think most people would place you. Look at the scale below and rate yourself in three levels: Low, Medium, and High.

Factor	Low	Medium	High
Extroversion			
Sociability			
Need for control			
Mental state (resilience)			
Professionalism/competence			
Personality (energy, charisma)			

to people in various situations?" This feedback is important because it may reveal the reasons you do or don't have the dream job or network you desire.

When you meet people, you should know how to present the best version of yourself - even when you're not 100% recharged, happy, and balanced. If you are unemployed, you might come across as someone who feels unjustly treated, and others will sense your toughness. The mini test above can help reveal areas where you need to improve. Compare your results to what your five advisors tell you.

Do you have a strong need for control? It's important to accept that when you network, you must give up some control. The people you meet will pick up on your signals and messages. From there, they may - or may not - become your advocates.

Networking is about letting people get to know you. The requirement for 70-100% openness scares many Type 8s and keeps them from networking. A typical Type 8 is personal but not private with others (and if they do open up, it usually takes time before they trust others enough to be completely open about their life, needs, dreams, etc.).

It takes courage to enter social relationships. You should feel secure in the social codes. As with any discipline, practice makes perfect. While you don't have to be private, being personal is a prerequisite for being an effective networker. Your network expects you to share your thoughts, challenges, considerations, and experiences. If you feel intimidated by direct dialogue because of the risk that people will form their own opinions about you, you may want to seek help to learn how to relax a bit more and loosen up.

Network type 9: "The comfortable networker"

Your self-perception is that you are peaceful, relaxed, calm, stable, mild, and gentle, but also stubborn, fixed, persistent, and sometimes unyielding.

If you are without a job, you're not necessarily worried or stressed about it (which many others might be). The reason is that many Type 9s have experienced life providing wonderful and grand opportunities without much effort, meaning you likely have a laid-back approach to life's challenges. You trust life and have an inner belief that everything will work out - and rightly so. You possess fundamental strong qualities that businesses seek.

Companies are increasingly looking for people with empathy, self-awareness, and social skills. A network-savvy Type 9 often embodies these qualities. The question is, are you network-savvy?

Characteristics of a type 9 networker

A typical Type 9 is a charismatic person who people generally enjoy being around. You are pleasant and approachable in a calm and relaxed way.

A typical Type 9 is viewed by those around them as gentle and accommodating. Your capacity for accommodation is very important when it comes to networking. To be a truly skilled networker requires mental energy, as the ability to accommodate other people demands a lot from you. Type 9 networkers often possess this capacity for accommodation.

A truly skilled networker is also tolerant, able to see others' differences as a source of inspiration. To attract and maintain relationships with people who are different from yourself, your starting point must be free of prejudice.

However, your comfort zone is your greatest challenge.

A small word of caution for you as a Type 9 is that you need to get better at handling change and being curious about what a new person or situation can bring.

In a global society with constant change, the status quo is always shifting. This creates a real need for collaboration between departments and between people. This is likely true at your workplace too. Cross-departmental collaboration - networking - lays the groundwork for innovation and improvement of the status quo. Networking can be the shortcut to optimizing your learning, development, and productivity.

Building a network requires interaction with people who work in different departments, positions, industries, etc., than your own. However, it's not always easy to get a Type 9 to step out when it comes to networking. Perhaps it's because you haven't yet felt the need to break free from your professional comfort zone. In other words, you haven't experienced being on a "burning platform."

A typical Type 9 loves a world that is unchanging, safe, and good. A typical Type 9 may struggle with appreciating development and change, preferring it to happen in small doses.

A typical Type 9 has a need to feel they belong to a group. In networking contexts, type 9s are driven by a sense of community and security. While this is possible, it can also be a challenge because a network evolves. People come and go in relationships. When thinking and working through relationships, you need to be prepared for the time and effort it requires, knowing that it won't always succeed. It takes energy because it involves people, and not all relationships are healthy for you. At heart, you believe that everyone has something good in them. You meet people with positivity.

As a Type 9, you may struggle to break off a relationship, even if it's not good for you. Type 9s tend to hold on to the present and may create an overly rosy picture of the people they surround themselves with.

A typical Type 9 is attracted to joining lodges or established networking groups because they offer a sense of unity and familiar routines, and you know who and what to expect. You likely enjoy meeting the same people repeatedly, allowing you to develop relationships at a pace that feels comfortable. You appreciate being around people who make you feel safe. You possess an inner calm that you prefer not to have disturbed by being exposed to too many new people at once. You enjoy building relationships at a pace that allows your soul to keep up.

The art of introductions

A while back, I was asked if I would consider writing about my journey - how I went from being a homeless foster care child to leading a tech startup in Silicon Valley. My answer was simple: Such a story would mostly be about others. The truth is, I am only here because someone took the time to introduce me. Someone made the call, wrote the email, or arranged the meeting that kicked the door open. A thoughtful, warm introduction - a powerful pitch on my behalf - made all the difference.

The transformative power of a warm introduction:

Have you ever been introduced to someone who changed your life? Maybe it was an introduction that landed you a job, secured funding for your startup, connected you with a business partner, or even led to a new home or a first date.

The impact of a well-crafted introduction is crucial. Sometimes it's the only way to access opportunities that otherwise feel out of reach. Research backs this up: According to a Harvard study, referrals are five times more likely to result in a job offer than applications submitted through other channels. Similarly, referred candidates are 55% faster to hire and stay longer in their roles. Introductions are more than just networking tools - they are bridges to new opportunities. Whether it's funding, partnerships, mentorship, or collaboration, introductions are often the hidden forces behind some of the most successful ventures.

The art and craft of a great introduction

In a world where LinkedIn, social media, and email make it easier than ever to ask for a connection, the quality of the introduction matters more than ever. A warm introduction acts as an endorsement - it lends trust and credibility to the person being introduced. But here's the catch: not every introduction works. How you introduce two people can determine whether they engage - or ignore the opportunity.

A good introduction is art. It requires intention, effort, and the ability to position both parties in a way that sparks interest. Here are a few key principles to get it right:

1. **Context is king:** A great introduction includes relevant context. Explain who each person is, why they should connect, and what makes the other person valuable. The better the context, the stronger the connection.

2. **Make it personal:** Tailor your introduction. Avoid sounding like a template - personalize it to both people. A sentence or two about shared interests or values can go a long way in making the introduction feel meaningful.

3. **Be brief, but impactful:** Keep your introduction concise. Include relevant achievements or key details without overloading the message. Attention is currency - so respect their time.

4. **Follow up and follow through:** A great introduction doesn't end with the first email or message. Check in on the progress and offer further help if needed. This shows genuine care and keeps the relationship warm.

Warm intros vs. cold outreach

Not every opportunity comes through a warm introduction. Sometimes you'll need to reach out cold - and that's okay. Cold outreach works, but only if it's done right. Research shows that emails with personalized subject lines are 26% more likely to be opened, and cold messages that are concise yet specific see higher response rates.

A cold outreach done well can open doors, but a warm introduction opens them wider and faster. In fact, warm introductions are often 20 times more effective than cold ones. Why? Because they carry trust - the trust of the person making the introduction.

Building a network of generous connectors

Over the years, I've been fortunate to surround myself with some of the most generous people on earth. They are masters of the art of introductions. These individuals have a passion for helping others succeed. They are thoughtful, intentional, and smart - they know how to make others shine.

Their introductions aren't transactional; they're transformational. They understand that every connection they facilitate has the potential to change someone's life.

Behind almost every successful partnership or venture is an introduction that made it possible. Sometimes it's pure luck - you sit next to the right person on a plane or bump into someone at an event. But often, success comes from intentional, well-crafted introductions.

The power of the pen (or chat, e-mail etc.) can open most doors in this world. But the question is: Do you know how to ask for an introduction? And do you know how to give one?

Whether you're introducing someone for a job, funding, or just a conversation, the way you do it matters. Thoughtful introductions build trust and momentum. And when done well, they can change lives.

Don't bother your network with requests and introductions all the time, and make sure there is a double opt in before you introduce two or more people to each other.

The importance of the double opt-in

One key element of mastering introductions is following the double opt-in policy - asking both parties for permission before connecting them. This step ensures the introduction is meaningful and welcomed, respecting everyone's time and boundaries.

Not every great person is the right match, and a misaligned introduction can do more harm than good. The double opt-in creates trust by making sure both sides are eager to engage, setting the stage for a productive relationship.

Thoughtful introductions create value

Introductions aren't just casual exchanges - they can change lives, open doors, and create opportunities that wouldn't happen otherwise. A thoughtful, well-executed introduction adds value and builds trust.

By embracing the double opt-in policy, you ensure introductions are intentional, meaningful, and effective. That small extra step might be the spark that turns a chance connection into something extraordinary. So be thoughtful. Be intentional. And always double opt-in. Because the right introduction, done right, doesn't just connect people - it creates opportunities that change lives. Always strive to make introductions mutually meaningful. Who knows - the next person you introduce could be the key to someone else's dream.

Invest in the art of introductions. Make it easy for others to help you by clearly communicating who you are, what you've accomplished, and where you're headed. Be strategic and generous with your connections. Be curious, ask questions, be of service, and lead with kindness. Stay prepared, have a vision, and go for it - because opportunities often come to those who are ready to act.

And remember: You don't need to meet everyone in person, host expensive lunches, or be the smartest person in the room to build an amazing network. A great network can be cultivated just as effectively online as in person. It's about intentionality, consistency, and authentic connection - not proximity.

Be proactive. When you show up with curiosity, vision, and generosity, the right people will naturally want to support and connect with you.

As we reach the end of the book

I want to emphasize that true networking is about so much more than just exchanging business cards or connecting on LinkedIn. It's about building authentic relationships that can transform both our personal and professional lives.

Throughout this book, I have shared my belief that networking should be approached with an open heart and a generous spirit. Each interaction we have is an opportunity to connect, to learn, and to uplift one another. The essence of networking lies not in what we can gain from others but in how we can support and contribute to their journeys.

A crucial aspect of this mindset is the concept of the +1. Whenever you receive an invitation to an event, always ask if you can bring a +1. Think about someone who could benefit just as much from that opportunity as you do. Networking is not about keeping others outside your power circle; it's about welcoming them in. By sharing opportunities, you help to cultivate a culture of generosity and inclusivity.

Remember the 70/30 rule: dedicate a portion of your conversations to sharing knowledge and professional insights while also allowing space for personal stories and connections. It is in these moments of vulnerability and openness that we forge the most meaningful relationships.

As you step into the world, let your networking efforts be guided by empathy and kindness. Seek to understand those around you and listen actively. Celebrate the diversity of experiences and perspectives that enrich our networks.

Together, we can create powerful ecosystems where everyone can thrive. Let us harness the power, wisdom, joy, and wealth that come from genuine connections. Grow, learn, and pass it on. As you move forward, I encourage you to connect with intention, embrace the stories of others, and remember that the true power of networking lies in the quality of the relationships we build.